TOO CUTE! BABY ANIMALS

Baby Dogs

by Colleen Sexton

Kaleidoscope
Minneapolis, MN

Where the Quest for Discovery Begins

This edition first published in 2024 by Kaleidoscope Publishing, Inc.

Kaleidoscope Publishing, Inc.
6012 Blue Circle Drive
Minnetonka, MN 55343

Library of Congress Control Number
2023936874

ISBN
978-1-64519-701-0 (library bound)
978-1-64519-749-2 (ebook)

Bigfoot Jr. lurks within one of the images in this book. It's up to you to find him!

Table of Contents

Puppies!

A mother dog gives birth. Her babies are puppies. A **litter** of puppies has a lot of brothers and sisters!

FUN FACT

There are about 400 breeds of dogs. They come in many shapes and sizes.

The mother licks the tiny puppies.
They start to breathe.

The puppies cannot hear or open their eyes. They smell their mother and snuggle close to her.

Newborn puppies make soft grunting sounds. They can bark when they are about three weeks old.

The puppies are hungry. They drink milk from their mother. It will make them strong.

Day One
cannot see or hear

Week One
sleeps a lot

Week Two
eyes open

The puppies curl up together to sleep. Sleeping helps them grow bigger and bigger!

FUN FACT
Newborn puppies sleep about 20 hours a day.

Week Three
can hear and walk

Week Four
teeth grow in

From Head to Tail

A puppy wiggles its furry body. It is awake and ready to play!

FUN FACT

Dogs have whiskers on their faces. These thick hairs help dogs find their way in the dark.

Fur keeps a dog warm. There are different colors and kinds of fur.

short coat

long coat

curly coat

coarse coat

soft coat

silky coat

Dogs wag their tails when they are happy!

The puppy wags its tail. The tail helps the puppy **balance** when it runs and jumps.

The puppy runs on padded paws. The front paws have five toes. The back paws have four. Each toe ends with a **claw**.

FUN FACT

Dogs sweat through their paws to cool off.

SNIFF! The puppy follows its nose. It has a super sense of smell.

FUN FACT

Every dog's nose makes a different print. It is like a human fingerprint.

The puppy's ears perk up. What is that noise? The puppy can move its ears to hear sounds from different directions.

Parts of a Puppy

Dog Facts

Kind of Animal: mammal

Size at Birth: from the size of a doughnut to the size of a loaf of bread

Litter Size: about three to nine puppies

Home: in people's homes as pets

A New Home

A puppy moves to a new home. Its owner will love the puppy and take care of it.

Puppies chew on toys and sticks when their adult teeth are coming in.

The puppy eats puppy food three times a day. It drinks fresh water. *SLURP!*

FUN FACT
Puppies are fully grown when they are one to two years old.

The puppy goes for walks. It runs and plays.

The puppy falls asleep on a soft bed. Good night!

Photo Glossary

balance: to stay steady; dogs need balance to land on all four paws when they run and jump.

breeds: groups of animals that have the same body features; the most popular dog breeds are Labrador retriever, French bulldog, golden retriever, German shepherd, and poodle.

claw: a sharp, curved nail at the end of an animal's toe

litter: a group of babies born at one time

mammal: a warm-blooded animal that has hair or fur; mammals drink their mother's milk.

whiskers: long, thick hairs that grow on an animal's face

Read More

Felix, Rebecca. *Good Dogs Only.* Minneapolis, Minn.: Lerner Publications, 2021.

Potts, Nikki. *Totally Amazing Facts About Dogs.* North Mankato, Minn.: Capstone Press, 2019.

Shanley, Margaret. *Baby Dogs.* Minneapolis, Minn.: Bearport Publishing, 2021.

Websites

FACTSURFER

Factsurfer.com gives you a safe, fun way to find more information.

1. Go to www.factsurfer.com.
2. Enter "Baby Dogs" into the search box and click 🔍
3. Select your book cover to see a list of related websites.

About the Author

Colleen Sexton is a writer and editor. She is the author of more than 100 nonfiction books for kids on topics ranging from astronauts to glaciers to elephants. She lives in Minnesota.

INDEX

PHOTO CREDITS

The images in this book are reproduced through the courtesy of: Natalia Fedosova/Shutterstock Images, cover; Dorottya Mathe/Shutterstock Images, title page, 17; Shutterstock Images, p. 3; Dmitry Kalinovsky/Shutterstock Images, p. 4–5; studio hoto/Shutterstock Images, p. 5; Rosa Jay/Shutterstock Images, p. 6 (top); Sbolotova/Shutterstock Images, p. 6 (bottom); Anna Hoychuk/Shutterstock Images, p. 7; rustycanuck/Shutterstock Images, p. 8; WilleeCole Photography/Shutterstock Images, p. 8–9; Natalia Fedosova/Shutterstock Images, p. 10; Rosa Jay/Shutterstock Images, p. 11 (silky coat); GPPets/Shutterstock Images, p. 11 (soft coat); GPPets/Shutterstock Images, p. 11 (coarse coat); Shutterstock Images, p. 11 (curly coat); cynoclub/Shutterstock Images, p. 11 (long coat); GoodFocused/Shutterstock Images, p. 11 (short coat); demanescale/Shutterstock Images, p. 12; Anna Hoychuk/Shutterstock Images, p. 13; Shutterstock Images, p. 14 (top); Javier Brosch/Shutterstock Images, p. 14 (bottom); anetapics/Shutterstock Images, p. 15; Jagodka/Shutterstock Images, p. 16; ANURAK PONGPATIMET/Shutterstock Images, p. 18 (top); Reddogs/Shutterstock Images, p. 18 (bottom); Nicky J Graham/Shutterstock Images, p. 19; Leszek Glasner/Shutterstock Images, p. 20–21; Chirtsova Natalia/Shutterstock Images, p. 21; demanescale/Shutterstock Images, p. 22 (balance); WilleeCole Photography/Shutterstock Images, p. 22 (breeds); Napat/Shutterstock Images, p. 22 (claws); ANURAK PONGPATIMET/Shutterstock Images, p. 22 (litter); Yuriy Bogatirev/Shutterstock Images, p. 22 (mammal); Annette Shaff/Shutterstock Images, p. 22 (whiskers); Patryk Kosmider/Shutterstock Images, p. 23.